FACT PLANET

ANIMALS AT RISK

IZZI HOWELL

Franklin Watts
First published in Great Britain in 2020 by the Watts Publishing Group
Copyright © the Watts Publishing Group 2020

Produced for Franklin Watts by
White-Thomson Publishing Ltd
www.wtpub.co.uk

Series Editor: Izzi Howell
Series Designer: Rocket Design (East Anglia) Ltd

HB ISBN: 978 1 4451 6921 7
PB ISBN: 978 1 4451 6922 4

Getty: Natalia Darmoroz 3b and 13b, davemantel 4b, MediaProduction 6b, PeJo29 9t, AnnstasAg 9b, Sloot 12br, vladsilver 16b, stanley45 24b; Shutterstock: Maquiladora, Maike Hildebrandt, Daria Riabets, natchapohn, iana kauri and robuart cover, HAP-PY-LUCKY title page and 7b, Natali Snailcat 3t and 6t, Vector Tradition 3c and 19b, Inspiring 4t, Maria Arts 5t, Maquiladora, Sunny_nsk and Olha1981 5b, MarcusVDT 7t, Nata Kuprova, eva_mask, A7880S, lukpedclub, MarySan, Alona Syplyak and SaveJungle 8, wildestanimal 9c and 28t, intararit 10t, oticki 10b, ActiveLines and maglyvi 11tl, Faber14 11tr, PhilipYb Studio 11b, Kletr 12t and 28b, MyImages – Micha 12bl, stas11 and Tartila 13t, Hennadii H 14t, Tsekhmister 14b, MakroBetz 15t, vectortatu, Gaidamashchuk and Drogatnev 15b, Tomacco 16t, Isabelle Kuehn 17tl and 29t, Abeselom Zerit 17tr, Good_Stock and Alfmaler 17b and 30, Macrovector 18t, costas anton dumitrescu and sub job 18b, TigerStock's 19t and 29cr, Joe Mercier 19c, Pierre-Yves Babelon 20t, HappyPictures 20b and 31t, Hennadii H 21t, Willyam Bradberry 21bl, cynoclub 21br and 29cl, Olha1981 and Daria Riabets 22t, Viktorija Reuta 22b, Marzolino 23t, Michael Fitzsimmons 23b, robuart 24t, Professional Bat 25t and 31b, Vladimir Wrangel 25b, Jen Watson 26t, KatePilko 26b, David Rasmus 27tl, Mix3r 27tr, 1000 Words Images 27b and 29b.

Every effort has been made to clear copyright. Should there be any inadvertent omission, please apply to the publisher for rectification.

The website addresses (URLs) included in this book were valid at the time of going to press. However, it is possible that contents or addresses may have changed since the publication of this book. No responsibility for any such changes can be accepted by either the author or the publisher.

All facts and statistics were correct at the time of press.

Printed in Dubai

Franklin Watts
An imprint of
Hachette Children's Group
Part of the Watts Publishing Group
Carmelite House
50 Victoria Embankment
London EC4Y 0DZ

An Hachette UK Company
www.hachette.co.uk
www.franklinwatts.co.uk

All **bold** words appear in the glossary on page 30.

Find the answers to all questions in this book on page 28.

Contents

Animals at risk

Many animals are at risk around the world.

Earth has been and is populated by many animals. However very few of all of these **species** are still alive today. They became **extinct** because of natural changes to our planet. For example, many scientists think that most of the dinosaurs became extinct after a giant asteroid hit Earth, which led to a change in Earth's **climate**.

However, today, human activity is the main reason why animals are at risk. We are destroying and polluting the **habitats** where animals live. The only way to save them is by changing our behaviour.

Many forests are being cut down (see pages 10–11), leaving forest animals without a home.

FACT!

99.9 per cent of all the species that have ever lived on Earth are now extinct!

We place animals at risk into different categories.

○ **Vulnerable**: animals slightly at risk

The African elephant is vulnerable (population: 415,000).

 At risk of extinction: animals at serious risk with a very low population

The Sumatran orang-utan is at risk of extinction (population: 14,000).

○ **Endangered**: animals at risk with a low population

The blue whale is endangered (population: 10,000–25,000).

 Extinct: animals that lived on Earth in the past but no longer exist any more

The quagga is extinct (population: 0).

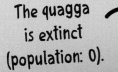

QUESTION TIME

WHICH OF THESE ANIMALS IS NOT ENDANGERED?

a Bengal tiger

b Green sea turtle

c European badger

Biodiversity

Biodiversity is the variety of animals and plants that live on Earth.

There is a huge variety of different habitats on Earth, such as the poles, woodlands, deserts, mountains, grasslands and the ocean. Different animal and plant species live in each habitat.

Each species has its own important role, either as food for other animals or as a **predator**. It is difficult for animals to live in less biodiverse habitats. With fewer species, there is not enough food to go around and some go hungry.

If the grasshopper population shrank, this frog would have less food to eat.

FACT!

The Amazon Rainforest in South America is one of the most biodiverse places on Earth. At least 10 per cent of all plant and animal species live there.

toucan

Many species are **adapted** to one habitat and can only live there. If a habitat is destroyed (see pages 10–11) or polluted (see pages 12–13), the animals that live there are at risk because they can't live anywhere else.

Food webs

If the population of one animal changes, it affects other animals in the habitat.

All of the living things in a habitat are connected. Animals eat plants and other animals for food. A diagram called a food web shows which animals depend on each other for food in a habitat.

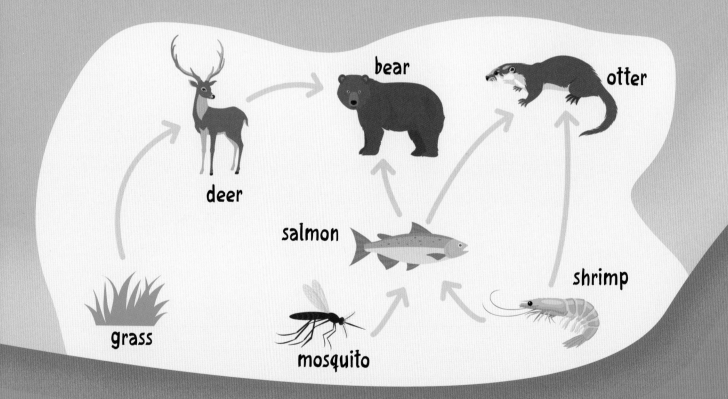

If the population of one animal in a food web gets smaller, such as the salmon above, it affects the entire food web. There will not be enough food for the animals that depend on salmon for food, such as the bear or the otter. These animals higher up the food web are at risk of going hungry and dying out.

The population of animals and plants below the animal at risk in the food web will also change. With fewer predators, fewer plants and prey are eaten. Their population may get bigger. This can have a negative effect on the environment. For example, a high number of insects may eat too many plants.

If there are too many caterpillars, there may not be enough plants to go around.

PICTURE PUZZLE

This animal is at the top of an ocean food web. What is it?

Habitat loss

Many habitats around the world are being destroyed.

Woodlands and rainforests are cut down. The trees are used for wood. Paths are cut through the forests so that new roads can be built. Many natural habitats are also cleared for farmland.

Even though plants grow on farms, they can't support the animals that lived in the habitat before its destruction. This is because **crops** aren't the right kind of food for these animals to eat. Crops also do not provide a place for animals to live.

Habitats are also cleared to build homes and businesses. As the human population on Earth grows, we need more space for people to live and work. However, destroying wild areas to create new towns is putting many animals at risk.

QUESTION TIME

MANY AREAS OF TROPICAL RAINFOREST ARE BEING CUT DOWN TO MAKE SPACE TO GROW ONE CROP. WHAT IS IT?

a Palm oil

b Carrots

c Corn

FACT!

Around half of the world's original forests have been destroyed.

Pollution

Humans are putting many animals in danger because of pollution.

Animals often get trapped in rubbish. This hurts them and makes it hard for them to move around. Some animals eat rubbish thinking that it is food. The rubbish damages the animal's stomach and insides, and can kill it.

PICTURE PUZZLE

This item of rubbish is very dangerous to animals, because they get their heads trapped in it. What is it?

FACT!

Scientists think that nearly every species of seabird eats plastic.

Air pollution from power plants, factories and vehicles leads to **acid rain**. When acid rain falls to the ground, it poisons plants, rivers and lakes. This is very dangerous for animals, as they eat the poison when they eat these plants or drink from these rivers or lakes.

Chemicals and waste are sometimes dumped in rivers and lakes. This poisons the fish and other animals that live there. Even if just one species is affected, the rest of the animals in the habitat will suffer too if the plants or animals they eat for food are killed.

Pesticides

Pesticides are useful for farmers but are harmful to animals.

Farmers use pesticides to protect their crops from insects that eat and damage the plants, such as caterpillars or beetles. However, pesticides kill any insects that live on or around the farm, including insects that are very important to plants, such as bees and butterflies.

Bees and butterflies are just some of the insects that **pollinate** plants. When they land on flowers to drink **nectar**, they pick up pollen. Bees and butterflies carry pollen from one plant to another. This is called pollination. Without pollination, plants could not **reproduce** and create new plants.

QUESTION TIME

WHICH WORD DESCRIBES CROPS THAT ARE GROWN WITHOUT PESTICIDES?

a Free-range

b Organic

c Luxury

One colony of **250,000** bees can pollinate **250 million** flowers in a day!

When bees and butterflies are killed by pesticides, plants are left unpollinated. This means that no fruit grows and there is less food for other animals in the habitat. So, many more animal species are at risk because of pesticides, not just bees and butterflies.

If no fruit grows, no seeds are produced and so no new plants will grow. This means that many animals will go hungry.

Climate change

Climate change threatens many animals.

Climate change is a change in temperature and weather on Earth. It is mainly caused by human activity and pollution. The temperature on Earth is getting warmer. This is making some habitats change so that it is harder for animals to live there.

Polar habitats are seriously affected by climate change. Warmer temperatures are making the ice melt. In the Arctic, there is no land, just ice. When the ice melts, there is nowhere for animals such as polar bears or ringed seals to rest or hunt.

PICTURE PUZZLE

This animal is at risk because of rising ocean temperatures. What is it?

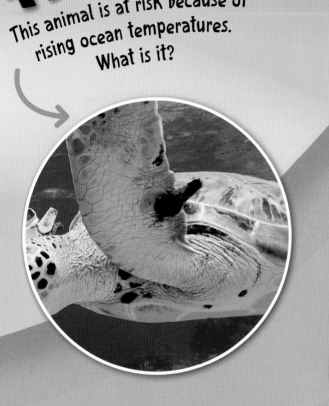

FACT!

If climate change continues, it could make **50 per cent** of all species alive today extinct by the year 2100.

Extreme weather, such as very hot and cold temperatures, **drought**, heavy rain and storms are killing plants in some habitats. This makes it hard for animals to live there, as there is no food for them to eat.

Hunting

Overhunting can affect animal populations.

Humans have always killed wild animals for food and other materials, such as their skin or fur. However, if we hunt too many animals and don't let their population recover, they can become vulnerable or endangered.

In prehistoric times, early humans had to hunt and eat animals to survive.

Nowadays, most meat comes from animals that live on farms. However, some people still kill wild animals for meat, materials or for sport. In some cases, this can be a good thing, as it stops the animal population from getting too high.

People often raise pheasants on farms to be hunted so that wild pheasant populations aren't affected.

PICTURE PUZZLE

Many animals are illegally killed for their fur. Which animal does this fur belong to?

FACT!

Every year, around
20,000
African elephants are illegally killed for their ivory.

Animal populations can get very low when people hunt them illegally (known as poaching) and don't follow the rules. **Poachers** often kill endangered animals, or large numbers of animals. African elephants are vulnerable because poachers kill them for their **tusks**, which are made of a **valuable** material called **ivory**.

Fishing

Many wild fish are caught for food.

Many people around the world depend on fish for food. This isn't a problem if they don't catch too many fish. However, this isn't always the case.

If fishing boats catch too many fish, or too many young fish, it hurts fish populations because the fish can't become adults and reproduce. People need to follow rules about the amount and size of the fish that they can catch. If they catch baby fish, they need to throw them back.

Some ways of fishing, such as using huge nets that drag along the ocean floor, are very dangerous. They kill other animals, such as dolphins, that won't be used for food. It is better for fishing boats to use smaller nets or fishing lines. In this way, they will only catch the fish that they need.

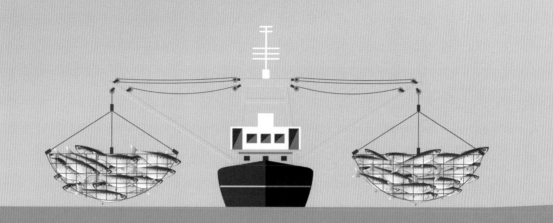

PICTURE PUZZLE

This fish is at risk from overfishing. Which fish is it?

Extinction

If we don't protect animals at risk, they can die out.

The Western black rhino became extinct in 2011.

The Tasmanian tiger became extinct in 1936.

Some species have recently become extinct in the 20th and 21st **centuries**. This is mainly due to overhunting and habitat loss.

The passenger pigeon became extinct in 1914.

However, if we don't act quickly enough, more species may disappear from our planet. We have to make changes to stop this from happening. See pages 26–27 for some ideas for how to protect animals.

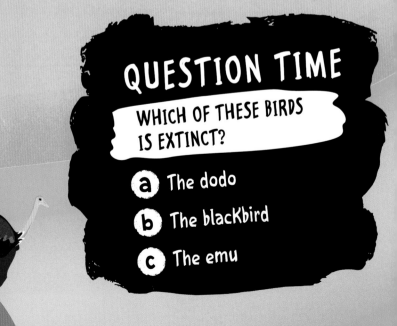

QUESTION TIME

WHICH OF THESE BIRDS IS EXTINCT?

a The dodo

b The blackbird

c The emu

Some species, such as the Guam kingfisher, are currently extinct in the wild. The only surviving members of the species live in zoos or **conservation areas**. There, they are safe from threats in their normal habitat, such as hunters. They can also reproduce to help keep the species alive.

FACT!

In the 19th century, the passenger pigeon was one of the most common birds in North America. Overhunting led to its extinction by 1914.

The only remaining Guam Kingfishers live in conservation areas.

Bringing animals back

Some animals have been saved from extinction!

There are different ways of helping animals that are very close to becoming extinct. We can raise them in safe spaces, such as zoos, and then bring them back to the wild when they are adults, so they have a better chance of surviving.

Some animals have been **reintroduced** into areas where they previously had become extinct. For example, the European beaver had become extinct in many areas of Europe. They only survived in eastern Europe, near Russia. Scientists took beavers from eastern Europe and brought them back to other European countries, such as the UK and Spain. Now beavers are no longer extinct in these countries.

Protecting animal habitats and stopping the threats that put them at risk can save animals from extinction. For example, in 2017, it was announced that giant pandas were no longer endangered, thanks to the creation of protected nature reserves for giant pandas to live in. Now they are only vulnerable. However, we need to continue to protect these species to make sure that their population continues to grow.

FACT!

In the 1930s, there were as few as 20 Siberian tigers, but by 2015, that number had grown to 540 tigers, thanks to conservation work.

QUESTION TIME

IN WHICH CONTINENT DO GIANT PANDAS LIVE?

a Africa

b South America

c Asia

Helping animals at risk

There are many ways to protect endangered animals.

The best way to help animals that are at risk is by solving the problems that are affecting them. For example, if an animal is affected by habitat loss, we can keep it safe by stopping the destruction of its habitat.

Politicians can make the biggest changes to help animals. They can pass laws to stop habitat destruction, reduce climate change and make hunting illegal. Find out what your local politician is doing to help or write them an email to ask for support. You could also organise a protest with a charity to raise awareness.

SAVE THE ELEPHANTS!

STOP CUTTING DOWN RAINFORESTS

PROTECT THE ENVIRONMENT

Scientists believe that only one law to protect endangered species saved 227 species in just 33 years!

There are also smaller actions that we can do to help animals. Walking or using public transport rather than cars is one way of helping to reduce climate change. Look out for products that are grown without destroying rainforests or fish caught without using dangerous nets.

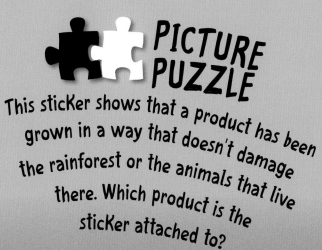

PICTURE PUZZLE

This sticker shows that a product has been grown in a way that doesn't damage the rainforest or the animals that live there. Which product is the sticker attached to?

Answers

PAGE 5

Question time!
c) European badger

PAGE 9

Picture Puzzle:
A great white shark

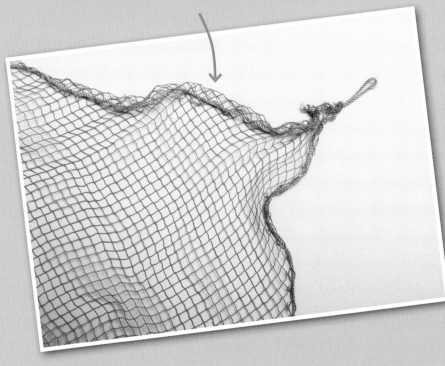

PAGE 11

Question Time!
a) Palm oil

PAGE 12

Picture Puzzle: A fishing net

PAGE 14

Question Time!
b) Organic

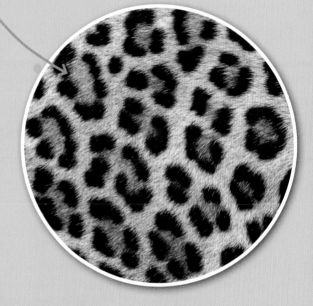

Glossary

acid rain rain containing poison caused by air pollution

adapted changed over time to become better suited

biodiversity the variety of different plants and animals that live in an area

century a period of one hundred years

climate the normal weather in an area

climate change the changes in weather on Earth

colony a group of the same animals that live together

conservation area an area where animals are protected

crops plants that are grown in large amounts for food, such as wheat

drought a period of time when there isn't enough water or rainfall

extinct if a species is extinct, it does not exist on Earth any more and won't be alive again

extreme unusual or very serious

habitat the natural area where an animal or plant lives

ivory the material that an elephant's tusk is made of

nectar a sweet liquid found in flowers

poacher someone who catches and kills animals illegally

pollinate when pollen is carried from plant to plant so that the plant can reproduce and make fruit

population the number of animals (or humans) living in an area, or on Earth

predator an animal that kills other animals for food

reintroduce to bring an animal back to live in an area where it used to live, but has died out

reproduce to produce young animals or plants

species a group of animals or plants with similar characteristics, such as a giant panda

tusk the long tooth of an animal, such as an elephant

valuable worth a lot of money

Further information

Books

Biodiversity (Ecographics)
by Izzi Howell (Franklin Watts, 2019)

Endangered Animals (Last Chance to See)
by Anita Ganeri (Wayland, 2019)

Endangered Wildlife series
by Anita Ganeri (Wayland, 2020)

Websites

www.natgeokids.com/uk/discover/animals/general-animals/extinct-animals/
Discover some fun facts about extinct animals.

www.bbc.co.uk/newsround/48611337
Learn more about animals that have been saved from extinction.

www.bbc.co.uk/cbbc/quizzes/endangered-species-quiz
Take a quiz about endangered animals.

Index